A THING OF BEAUTY IS

A JOY FOR EVER:

ITS LOVELINESS INCREASES;

IT WILL NEVER

PASS INTO NOTHINGNESS.

— JOHN KEATS —

THE
GIFTED BUTTON

Fashion Buttons Into
Gorgeous Gifts
And Wearable Art

JUDITH MAAS RHEINGOLD

ILLUSTRATIONS BY

CATHERINE ROSE CROWTHER

HEARST BOOKS
NEW YORK

*This book could not have been written
without the help of Catherine Rose Crowther, Christine Carswell,
Aaron Stapley, and Esther Mitgang. A special thank you
to those who graciously allowed me to raid their private
button collections: Jim Dutra, Thea Schrack,
Babe Rae, Helen Sjolander, Patricia Stapley Charlton,
Gerri Levine, and Elise Vagadori.*

〜

〜

It is the policy of William Morrow and Company, Inc.,
and its imprints and affiliates, recognizing the importance of
preserving what has been written, to print the books we publish
on acid-free paper, and we exert our best efforts to that end.

〜

Library of Congress Catalog Number:
LC 92-74582

Printed in Singapore

First Edition
1 3 5 7 9 10 8 6 4 2

DEDICATED TO

~ MY DARLING NIECES ~

CATHERINE KEANE CROWTHER

AND

CLAIRE ELIZABETH CROWTHER

CONTENTS

THE FUN ART OF BUTTON CRAFT

✂ I am a faithful keeper of the button, the latest in a long line of devotees. When I was a child, I was fascinated by my grandmother's round cookie tin filled to brimming with buttons. There were hundreds of them. Like many of her friends, she'd started collecting and saving them in the 1930s. Her pockets were empty, but where others saw only an ordinary button, she saw something of value, a miniature work of art.

I never tired of playing with her collection. I'd tumble out her tin, chock-full of buttons, and sit on the living room floor, a castaway in a sea of notions. Time seemed to melt away and by the end of the afternoon, I had organized my bounty into neat rows, ready to be pasted onto cards. In the most special row were my very favorite buttons: an antelope etched in silver, a tiny wreath of roses under glass, abalone disks that changed from pink to blue to green. I can remember examining each one, turning it over in my hand, and wondering how something so small could be so fine and beautiful.

I inherited those tiny treasures, and, over the years, I've added jewels of my own — the little pearl buttons from a robe my daughter wore as a baby, a stately Art Deco pair I discovered on vacation one summer, and an elegant set of leather-braided buttons from a Savile Row topcoat of my husband's. Now my collection holds as many memories as an heirloom quilt. To me, it's priceless.

I realize how lucky I am to have my grandmother's trove passed down to me. But I also envy those of you who are just about to begin your quest for the Perfect Button. What a thrill to light triumphantly upon a one-of-a-kind vintage button at a flea market, or to come upon a sparkling matched pair in a secondhand store! A button doesn't have to be an antique to be a work of art.

I began experimenting with restyling my well-worn, but favorite items of clothing. Nothing refreshes like a brand-new set of buttons. Yet, the day finally came when I had changed all the buttons on my family's clothing and I realized my button craft was destined for greater things. Believing, like the Gypsies, that buttons bring good fortune, I began making fashion accessories, wearable art, and decorative home furnishings. I button-bespangled jewelry, buttonized picture frames, lamp shades, mirrors, and jars, and turned them into marvelous gifts. Even the dog received her own rhinestone-button collar and leash.

All of the gifts in *The Gifted Button* are wonderfully fun and easy to craft at home. The projects call for the two basic button types: sew-through, which have two holes or four holes; and shank buttons,

Shank

Two-Hole

Four-Hole

Novelty

Metallic

Picture

which have a loop on the underside. Buttons are made from virtually every kind of material — wood, mother-of-pearl, glass, shell, leather, horn and bone, enamel, plastic, and metals with the aura of precious ores. Catherine Rose's painting beautifully illustrates the amazing variety you have to choose from. We have organized them into the six categories used in the book: shanks, two-hole, four-hole, novelty buttons (also known as goofies or realistics), metallics, and picture buttons. I adore them all and could never name my favorite.

Select your buttons with care and consideration. For special friends, take time to find the signature button that seems to capture their personality or reflect a hobby. Never scorn a shirt button! The humble plastic two-hole can be as appropriate as the finest filigree.

One of the best things about buttons is how simple they are to work with. There are no complicated crafting techniques to learn. All the buttons in these projects are either sewed on, wired together, or affixed with glue. I recommend Aleene's plastic-safe tacky glue, a permanent bonding adhesive that dries quickly to clear and won't damage plastic. In case you have difficulty finding any of the craft supplies needed, "The Button Lover's Source Guide" at the back of the book lists reliable mail-order suppliers around the country.

These beautiful handmade keepsakes deserve to be presented with special care. I think your friends will appreciate the gift-wrapping touches I have fashioned to complement each project.

Buttons change hands for hundreds of dollars now. But I invest in them for the love and friendship these gifted buttons bring me. So dust off your own tin of buttons, scour your neighborhood haberdasher's and antique shops, and dive in. The bedazzling world of buttons awaits you.

THE GIFTED BUTTON

BEAUTY AND THE BUTTON

✂ The vanity set is back in vogue, recalling a time gone by when a woman's toilette was leisurely and elegant. Refresh your lip gloss and powder your nose in the diffused glow of the Pearl-Light Lamp. It will set the radiant bouquet of buttons decorating the Crystal Garden Hand Mirror and Vanity Pot to dancing. The glistening trio is perfectly displayed with a treasure trove of crystal bottles and silvery flacons.

Pearl-Light Lamp Shade

✂ The centerpiece in a jumble of frivolous necessities, the Pearl-Light Lamp Shade is button-encrusted with hundreds of mother-of-pearl, soft-white bone, and sweet-cream-colored buttons. The shade is exquisite by day or night. With the light from a forty watt bulb (not more than a sixty-watt, please, or you will burn the shade) shining through, it's an underwater sunbeam. Turn the light off, it's the surface of a cay beach after a tropical storm. Here's your chance to find a use for all the odd white buttons you've stashed away.

Raid your sewing basket for two-hole, four-hole, and orphan shanks. Supplement if necessary with buttons sold on cards at notions stores, secondhand shops, and variety stores. Men's oxford-cloth shirt buttons are perfect. The shade size is standard to a candlestick-style, single-bulb lamp.

> *Fabric lamp shade, acrylic-lined, soft white,*
> *   4 inches high x 5 inches diameter*
> *Tube dry-to-clear, plastic-safe glue*
> *48 sew-through buttons, 1/4 inch diameter*
> *58 assorted sew-through and shank buttons,*
> *   1/2 inch diameter*
> *24 assorted sew-through and shank buttons,*
> *   3/4 inch diameter*
> *24 assorted sew-through and shank buttons,*
> *   7/8 inch diameter*
> *4 assorted shank buttons, 1 1/2 inches diameter*
> *26 assorted shank buttons, dome-shaped, 3/8 inch diameter*
> *26 assorted shank buttons, dome-shaped, 1/2 inch diameter*

✂   At the top rim of the shade, glue a band of twenty-four quarter-inch sew-through buttons to fit tightly next to each other. At the bottom rim of the shade, glue a band of thirty-four half-inch assorted sew-through and shank buttons to fit tightly next to each other, overlapping when a shank abuts a sew-through. Set aside to dry for thirty minutes.

✂   Divide the remaining buttons into four groups. Each group contains a one-and-one-half-inch shank and an assortment of sew-throughs and shanks, varying in size. To visually organize your design, imagine the shade divided into four "fan-shaped" sections.

✂   Glue a large shank in the center of the first section to act as an anchor for the design. Glue buttons all around it, placed to fit tightly next to each other: a tiny snuggled against a large, a sew-through peeking out from behind a shank, two shanks vying side-by-side, a dome shape dominating a flat. When you have completely button-encrusted the section, lay the shade on the opposite side to dry, about thirty minutes.

✂   Repeat the gluing and drying process to button-frost the shade. Survey your artwork. Glue tiny buttons to cover any bare spots betwixt and between. Stand the shade upright and set it aside to dry overnight.

Crystal Garden Hand Mirror And Vanity Pot

✂   Shimmering sea flowers in a forest of lacy coral, the Crystal Garden Hand Mirror and Vanity Pot are a laureate of multi-faceted glass shank buttons clustered in the center of a lovelace appliqué. The lace-and-colored-glass combination is a marriage made in heaven. All of the buttons are shank, faceted glass to capture light, in gem hues ranging from ruby red, emerald green, and sapphire blue to their watery pastel counterparts of amethyst,

4

tourmaline, and aquamarine. A top-notch notions store will have an inspiring variety of faux-lace appliqués. The appliqué dominates the design, so pick a faux-lace pattern both ornate and detailed to support the shimmering button bouquet.

> *2 matching faceted clear-glass shank buttons, mirror back,*
> *1 inch diameter*
> *2 matching black shank buttons, rhinestone center,*
> *3/4 inch diameter*
> *2 matching faceted green-glass shank buttons,*
> *3/4 inch diameter*
> *2 matching faceted amethyst-glass shank buttons,*
> *triangle-shaped, 3/4 inch wide*
> *2 metallic shank buttons, flower-shaped, rhinestone center,*
> *3/4 inch diameter*
> *6 faceted jewel-colored glass shank buttons,*
> *1/2 inch diameter*
> *14 faceted jewel-colored glass shank buttons (seven*
> *matching pairs), 1/4 inch diameter*
> *Lace appliqué, cream-colored, 5 inches diameter*
> *Hand mirror, light wood, 11 inches long (mirror diameter*
> *5 1/2 inches)*
> *Tube dry-to-clear, plastic-safe glue*
> *Glass vanity pot, light-wood lid, 4 inches diameter*
> *Lace appliqué, cream-colored, 3 1/2 inches diameter*

✂   Divide the buttons into two identical groups so the hand mirror and jar lid match.

✂   To decorate the back of the mirror, place a dollop of glue in the center. Turn the appliqué over, design side down, and run a circle of glue around the edge. Turn it right side up to glue in place. Nudge the appliqué's edges into the middle a bit to force the material to pucker up, giving the lace some extra dimension. Set aside to dry for thirty minutes.

✂   Glue the one-inch button to the center of the appliqué. Arrange crystal-centered black button, an emerald-green, an amethyst triangle, a metallic flower, and three mixed jewel-colored buttons to ring the central button. Glue them down to touch and overlap, forming a chunky cluster. Position seven quarter-inch jewel-colored buttons around the edges of the cluster and in between the larger buttons as twinkling accents. Glue them in place. Set aside to dry overnight.

✂   Repeat this procedure to decorate the lid of the vanity pot. Set aside to dry overnight.

✂   To present this Vanity Fare, individually wrap each item in white tissue, including the lamp base. Nest them in a large Tiffany-blue gift box, size determined by the length of the lamp base. Stuff extra tissue around to cushion and protect the gift of pearls and gems. Tie a white satin ribbon, bundle-style, for a final flourish.

BUTTONED DOWN AND BEST DRESSED

✄ Raffishly attractive at lapel and cuff, the Fleur-de-Lys Buttoniere and Button-Coupled Cuff Links will put a bounce in the step of any wing-tipped pinstripe (and set the hips to swinging of any sling-backed houndstooth) about town. Embossed with wonderful symbols from nature and the supernatural, the military-chic of these metallic accessories are extra fun to present in the gold-finished Buttoned-Down Gift Box.

Fleur-de-Lys Buttoniere

✄ Like a royal crest, the Fleur-de-Lys Buttoniere sports buttons both mystical and traditional. The regal shape of a fleur-de-lys is a stately foil to an honor guard of round gold medallions. Suspended beneath your distinctive emblem dangle three chunky stacks of two-hole buttons, colored metallics of precious old gold, bronze, and platinum. It's hard to believe that this wearable sculpture begins with a blanket pin!

24 yards gold-metal wire, 28 gauge
Wire nippers
Gold-metal blanket pin, 2 inches long
Gold-metal shank button, satin finish, 3/4 inch diameter
Gold-metal shank button, satin finish, 5/8 inch diameter
17 assorted metallic two-hole buttons, 1/2 inch to
    5/8 inch diameter
Gold-metal two-hole button, dome-shaped,
    1/2 inch diameter
2 matching gold-metal shank buttons, 3/8 inch diameter
Gold-metal shank button, fleur-de-lys, 1 inch long
Tube dry-to-clear, plastic-safe glue

✄   Cut a length of wire with your nippers, about seven inches. Hold the blanket pin front side up, with the pin opening at the top, and position the three-quarter-inch shank to cover the clasp. Thread the wire through the shank, and then wrap it around the clasp of the pin to secure the button firmly in place. Keep threading the wire, neatly and evenly, through the shank and around the clasp until all the wire is used, making sure, though, that the pin is free to open.

✄   Cut a second length of wire, about seven inches. Position the five-eighths-inch shank to cover the pin's tail end and repeat the procedure of threading on.

✄　Divide the flat two-hole buttons into three groups of six, seven, and four buttons. Distribute the buttons with an eye toward variety of size and metallic hue.

✄　To assemble the right-hand hanging stack of buttons, cut a length of wire, about fifteen inches. Fold it in half, and then in half again, to form a double-stranded U-shape. Begin by attaching the dome-shaped two-hole button. Thread the left end of the wire through the left hole of the button and the right end through the right hole. Slide the button down to cradle in the center of the U. Thread the group of six buttons on, one at a time, in the same way. To finish the stack, thread both ends of wire through the shank of a three-eighths-inch button. Press all the buttons down firmly to pack the stack. Wrap the remaining wire around the bottom rung of the pin to fit snugly against the tail button.

✄　To assemble the middle stack of seven buttons, cut another length of wire, about fifteen inches. Repeat the procedure, crowning the stack with the fleur-de-lys. Wrap the wire around the bottom rung of the pin to nestle against the right-hand stack.

✄　To assemble the left-hand stack of four, cut a final length of wire, about fifteen inches. Repeat the procedure, topping the stack with a three-eighths-inch shank. Wrap the wire around the bottom rung of the pin to secure the stack as before, nudging it against the large shank concealing the clasp.

✄　Place a dollop of glue behind the large shanks covering the clasp and tail end of the pin. Set aside overnight to dry.

Button-Coupled Cuff Links

✂ Fashioned from the same crested metallics embellishing the buttoniere, these debonair cuff links are crafted in seconds using small metal loops called findings. I buy these nifty items by the bag at my local notions store. They're great to have on hand to accessorize an outfit at a moment's notice.

Needle-nose pliers
4 matching gold-metal shank buttons, 5/8 inch diameter
Pair cuff-link findings

✂ Use the needle-nose pliers to gently pry open both ends of the finding. Slide a shank button over each end of the finding to fit in the open loop. Squeeze the ends of the finding closed, securing the buttons in place. Repeat the process to create the second cuff link.

Buttoned-Down Gift Box

✂ Showcase your gifts in a wonderful Directoire box studded with five gold medallions cushioned in moire-ribbon roses. In years to come, this elegant receptacle may be the home for favorite recipes or treasured bijoux. For the moment, let it convey your Buttoniere and Cuff Links with all the pomp and splendor they deserve.

6 x 10-inch box with hinged top, unfinished wood,
*   4 inches deep*
Paintbrush, 1 inch wide
Bottle gold-leaf paint
25 inches dark green moire French wire ribbon,
*   1 inch wide*
Gold-metal shank button, 1 inch diameter
4 gold-metal shank buttons, 3/4 inch diameter
Tube dry-to-clear, plastic safe glue
7-inch piece corrugated cardboard, 3 inches wide
7-inch sheet rubber foam, 3 inches wide x 1/4 thick
8 inches dark green moire silk, 4 inches wide
2 tiny gold-colored safety pins

✂   Paint the box inside and out with gold leaf. Set aside overnight in a cool, dry place.

✂   Cut the French wire ribbon into equal lengths, each about five inches.

✂   To create a ribbon rosette, expose the wire along the top of the ribbon by gently pushing the material back at both ends. Twist the ends together, gathering the ribbon into a ruffle. Repeat the process at the bottom, exposing the wire, pushing the material back to ruffle, and twisting the wire ends to complete your open-centered ribbon rosette. Repeat this process to create four more rosettes.

✂ To attach the rosettes and the medallions to the lid of the box, place a dollop of glue in the center of the lid. Position a rosette on top of the glue and crown the center with the one-inch button. Gently press the button down to make contact with the glue. Repeat the procedure to glue a rosette and a button at each corner of the lid.

✂ Dot the corrugated cardboard with glue, and paste on the rubber foam. Place the silk on a flat surface. Position the cardboard, foam side down, on top of the material. Fold the overlapping ends over the back of the cardboard and glue in place. Set aside to dry, about four hours.

✂ Pin the buttoniere to the center of the silk-covered cardboard. Position a cuff link on either side, pinned in place with tiny gold safety pins.

✂ Corrugated cardboard is extremely flexible. Bend the sides down, about one inch at each end to fit snugly in the box. Press it into the box to ride about one inch from the rim.

BUTTONS ARE A DOG'S BEST FRIEND

✂ The Pampered Pet Collar and Leash are the ultimate in canine chic. Buttonizing this elegant tether is so fast and easy, your motley mutt will be transformed into a Park Avenue pooch in the twinkle of an eye. The rhinestone and glass gleamers will bow-wow even Ruff Lauren's owner, who'll never suspect you whipped up this glamorous gift between brunch and cocktails.

Pampered Pet Collar And Leash

✂ I wanted rhinestone buttons, all shiny and new, mixed with vintage diamantés in silvery settings to match our beloved Westie's sparkling personality. Contrasting the glitter, the choice of color for the leash and collar is obvious, The Classic Basic Black. The Pampered Pet Collar and Leash were designed to fit my medium-size darling. Consider the pup you're outfitting. Add or subtract buttons from my instructions to accommodate the size of the collar and length of the leash. The collar looks best with the buttons separated

by a one-inch space; the leash with the buttons spaced two inches apart.

> *13 assorted rhinestone shank buttons, 1/2 inch diameter*
> *14 assorted rhinestone shank buttons, 3/8 inch diameter*
> *Black woven-nylon collar, 5/8 inch wide x 14 inches long*
> *Measuring tape*
> *Spool black cotton thread, heavy-duty*
> *Standard sewing needle, eye-size to accommodate thread*
> *1 black woven-nylon leash, 47 inches long*

✄   Divide the buttons into two groups. Select six half-inch buttons and six three-eighths-inch buttons for the collar. Select seven half-inch buttons and eight three-eighths-inch buttons for the leash.

✄   To fashion the collar, start with a half-inch button. Place it two inches from the buckle and about one-half inch from the leash loop. Center it on the width of the band. Sew it down. Select a three-eighths-inch button. Place it one inch from the first button, center it on the width of the band, and sew it down. Repeat this procedure to attach the remaining buttons, alternating sizes, and maintaining the one-inch space between each button. As you choose each button, juxtapose shapes and sparkle quality for optimum design impact. The last button will position about one inch from the collar's tightest notch-hole.

✄   To bejewel the leash, start with a three-eighths-inch button.

Place it three inches from the claw-hook clasp. Center it on the width of the band. Sew it down. Select a half-inch button. Place it two inches from the first button, center it on the width of the band, and sew it down. Repeat this procedure to attach the remaining buttons, alternating sizes and maintaining the two-inch space between each button. The last button will position about one inch from the seam where the leash loops to form the handle.

✂   To present the very lucky layabout with his or her doggone perfect gift, dress a floppy doggie doppelgänger in the Pampered Pet Collar and Leash.

CUTE AS
A BUTTON

✂ Pink elephants, calico kittens, sporty checkerboards, and funny faces — novelty buttons, sometimes called goofies or realistics, are designed to make us smile. The Button-Adorned Child's Denim Jacket and matching Button & Bow Baseball Cap display a crazy quilt of colored buttons in all their glory. I guarantee you'll have as much fun finding the fanciful theme buttons as your child will have wearing this artful ensemble.

Button-Adorned Child's Denim Jacket

✂ Create a button scheme that will especially appeal to your child. My daughter, Mamie, and I planned this jacket on our vacation in Paris. We wandered the flea market and browsed in tiny shops collecting a bright harvest of shank buttons to sew on the sleeves of her favorite jacket.

> *86 assorted novelty shank buttons, 3/4 inch to*
> *1/2 inch diameter*
> *Blue denim jacket, size appropriate*

Spool black cotton thread, heavy-duty
Standard steel needle, eye-size to accommodate thread

✂ Divide your buttons into two groups of forty-three, a balanced mix of sizes, shapes, and colors. I suggest you arrange the buttons on a side table to plan your design before you start to sew the buttons on the sleeves.

✂ Select three buttons from each group to decorate the collar points. Set them aside for last.

✂ Begin by sewing the buttons on one of the sleeves. Position the first button to align with the chest seam, clearing the shoulder seam by about one-half inch. Follow the semicircular curve of the armhole to sew five more buttons in place, spacing them about one inch apart. The sixth button should position to align with the shoulder-blade seam.

✂ Use the six buttons framing the armhole to establish an invisible diagonal grid running down the length of the sleeve. A carefree staggered effect is the most pleasing, always evenly spaced. Referring to these button space-markers for guidance, sew the rest of the buttons down the length of the arm. Leave the cuffs bare so they can be turned back easily, and avoid sewing buttons to the underside of the arms, also for comfort.

✂ Repeat this process to sew the buttons on the other sleeve.

✂ Sew three buttons to each collar, starting at the point and working toward the back, spaced about one inch apart.

Button & Bow Baseball Cap

✂ I guarantee that heads will turn as your child skips down the street wearing this playful hat! Primary-colored two-hole buttons, including a few startling white, make a striking contrast to the bright red cap. Tiny bow knots, instead of stitches, tie the buttons pertly in place.

> 6 two-hole buttons, 1 inch diameter
> 12 two-hole buttons, 3/4 inch diameter
> 12 two-hole buttons, 1/2 inch diameter
> 6 novelty two-hole buttons, 3/4 inch diameter
> 7 yards red satin ribbon, 1/16 inch wide
> Red worsted-wool baseball cap, size appropriate
> Embroidery needle, eye-size to accommodate ribbon
> Tube dry-to-clear, plastic-safe glue
> Toothpicks

✂ The classic baseball cap has six triangular sections, so divide your buttons into six groups of six, matching the sizes in each.

✂ Cut the ribbon into thirty-six lengths, each seven inches. Thread your needle with the first length. Don't knot the ribbon.

✂ Position a three-quarter-inch button at the narrow point of one section. Push the needle through the top of the right buttonhole to emerge inside the cap. Hold the ribbon tail to prevent it from being drawn through the buttonhole and into the cap. Turn the cap

20

inside out and poke the needle through the left hole, drawing the ribbon out the top of the button. Both ends of the ribbon are now hanging outside the cap. Slide the needle off the ribbon. Pull the ends of the ribbon to equal lengths, tie them together tightly, and make a bow to fasten the button in place securely. Continue to bow-sew the five other buttons in the same way, staggering their alignment, juxtaposing colors, varying the sizes, and mixing shapes. Repeat this process to cover the cap in buttons and bows.

✄ Survey your handiwork. Snip the ribbon ends to uniform lengths. A tiny dab of glue, applied with a toothpick to the center of each bow, will make the cap kid-proof. Hang the cap on a wine bottle or a hatrack in a cool place to dry overnight.

✄ What could be more natural than to use a backpack as your gift wrapping? You can glue a giant button on the flap as a tie-in, too.

THE LANGUAGE
OF BUTTONS

✂ Are you, like me, an avid reader?
I finish one book just to begin another. Novels and true crime, poetry
and politics, I always carry my current read with me to take advan-
tage of special times during the day when I can dip in. The Bold and
the Beautiful Book Jacket is a portable home for your best friend with
a Big Button Bookmark to mark the spot.

The Bold And The Beautiful Book Jacket

✂ This homespun gift was inspired by a friend in my monthly
reading group. She's a true bibliophile. We lend books to each other
all the time, and mine were looking the worse for wear. Some people
are especially hard on paperbacks. I decided that the next time I lent
her a book from my library, I would protect it from this voracious
reader in a reusable book jacket. I turned a book into a pocketbook
for selfish reasons, I guess.

19 inches aqua-green felt, double-weight, 4 inches wide
12-inch metal ruler

Scissors

18 x 24-inch sheet graph paper, 1/4 grid

Straight pins

Pencil

Pinking shears

17 inches navy-blue felt, double-weight, 8 1/2 inches wide

Sewing machine

Spool navy-blue cotton thread

Steel-head hammer

Phillips-head screwdriver

28 inches navy-blue satin cording, 3/8 inch wide

Scotch tape

Standard steel needle, eye-size to choice

Yellow bakelite shank button, flower-shaped or sunburst,
   1 1/2 inches diameter

12 matching yellow shank buttons, dome-shaped,
   1/2 inch diameter

✄   Begin by creating the aqua-green zigzag flashes that will decorate the book jacket.

✄   Cut two inches off the length of the felt with scissors. Set it aside for later.

✄   Cut the felt in half lengthwise, making two rectangular strips, seventeen inches long by two inches wide. Lay the strips horizontally on a flat work surface.

✂ Cut a piece of graph paper to measure seventeen inches long by two inches wide to act as a template. Pin a piece of graph paper to one of the felt strips. With your ruler, measure three quarters of an inch down from the top edge toward the center and draw a seventeen-inch pencil line along the length of the paper. Measure three quarters of an inch up from the bottom edge of the paper and draw a second pencil line the same length. Starting at the top-left corner, measure off one inch along the top and mark it with a pencil dot. Continue along the top edge, placing dots every two inches. Move down to the upper-center line and place a pencil dot at the left edge. Continue along the line, placing dots two inches apart. Move down to the lower-center line, measure one inch in from the left, and place a pencil dot. Continue along the line, placing dots every two inches. Move to the bottom edge; place a dot at the left edge. Continue along the line, placing dots two inches apart.

✂ Draw a diagonal line from the dot at the far left edge of the upper-center line to the first dot on the top line above it. Turn your ruler to point down, and connect that dot with the dot diagonally below it on the upper-center line. Turn your ruler to point up, and connect that dot with the next dot at the top diagonally above it. By now you will see a zigzag emerging along the top edge of the strip. Continue to draw diagonal lines, connecting the dots along the top with their corresponding dots on the upper-center line. Draw the lines in the same way to create the bottom edge of the zigzag, connecting the dots marked on the bottom edge with their corresponding dots on the lower-center line. Cut along the pencil lines with the pinking shears to create the first zigzag flash.

✂ Unpin the graph paper and reattach it to the other felt strip. Use it as a template to cut out the second zigzag flash.

✂ Lay the navy-blue felt horizontally on your work surface. Place the two flashes along the length of the blue felt. Flip the bottom one over to mirror the top one. Position them two inches apart. They should appear to center top and bottom on the width of the book jacket. Pin them in place. Sew them down, using a loose zigzag stitch on your sewing machine, one-quarter inch from the edges. If you prefer to hand-sew this project, a simple running stitch will work nicely.

✂ To create the center ornament, trim the two-inch piece of aqua felt with the pinking shears to measure one-and-one-half inches square. Turn sideways to make a diamond. Pin in place to position five inches from the right edge of the book jacket, centered between the flashes. Sew it down a quarter-inch in from the edges with a zigzag stitch.

✂ Turn the jacket over, inside facing you. Fold the side ends over, three-and-one-half inches. Pin them closed at top and bottom. Using a straight stitch on your machine, or a tight running or blanket stitch if you are sewing the gift by hand, sew shut along the top and bottom, one-half inch in from the edges. Trim the top and bottom edges, about one-quarter inch, with the pinking shears.

✂ Protect your worktable to avoid damage to the surface as you hammer the holes through the felt for the tote handles. Turn the jacket, decorated side up. Place a pencil dot about half an inch in from the left side of the upper flash and a corresponding one on the bottom flash. The dots should align and be centered within the zigzag. Repeat, top and bottom, at the right side. Place your screwdriver over one of the dots. Hit it with the hammer. One shot should be enough to make a hole through the layers of felt. Make the rest of the holes in the same way.

✂ Cut the cording in half. Wrap tape around the four tips to prevent them from fraying and to ease insertion. Start at the right side of the jacket. Thread a cord end through the hole in the upper flash. Insert it from back to front. Remove the tape. Tie the end into a chunky knot. Insert the other end through the hole on the lower flash in the same way. Remove the tape and tie into a chunky knot. Repeat the process to create the handle on the opposite end of the jacket.

✂ Finish decorating the jacket with lovely buttons. Position the flower-shaped, or sunburst, button on the centerpiece of aqua felt. Sew it in place to perch centered on the diamond.

✂ Arrange the twelve dome-shaped shank buttons, six on

the front and six on the back. Position three on the upper flash and three on the lower flash. Sew them in place to sit centered in the crooks of the zigzags. Repeat the process to decorate the back of the jacket.

Big Button Bookmark

✄   Even the most zealous reader occasionally takes a break (if only to sleep), so a bookmark is simply essential. A traditional wide ribbon, enhanced with a single spectacular button, does the job perfectly.

> *12 inches navy-blue moire grosgrain ribbon,*
> *   1 1/2 inches wide*
> *Navy-blue cotton thread*
> *Standard steel needle*
> *Two-hole button, abalone shell, 1 inch diameter*
> *Shank button, flower-shaped or sunburst,*
> *   1 1/2 inches diameter*
> *Pinking shears*

✄   Make a one-inch fold at the top end of the ribbon. Double it back on itself one inch to create a stable backing for the buttons. Position the two-hole button on top of the folded ribbon and sew it in place. Turn the ribbon over. Sew the shank button to the front.

Place it opposite the two-hole, supporting it from behind.

✂ Using your pinking shears, cut a triangle about one-inch deep at the bottom of the ribbon to create a pennant finish.

✂ Complete your gift by tucking the latest best-seller into the Bold and the Beautiful Book Jacket. Inscribe the title page, slip in the bookmark, billow in tissue, and pop it into a canvas bookbag.

One Two Button My Shoe and a Bangle Bracelet, Too

✂ A glint of gold on your wrist and a twinkle of gold on your toes dramatically accessorize a Day-to-Evening ensemble. After five, you can turn a business suit into a dinner suit by slipping on the Gold Button Bangle Bracelet and clipping the Gold Button Shoe Ornaments to your basic black pumps. The style is classic. The look is elegant. The effect is stunning.

Gold Button Bangle Bracelet

✂ You will enjoy selecting the buttons for this ultralux piece of jewelry. Choose an exciting assortment of patterns, textures, and shades of gold. The metal buttons will make a wonderful tinkling sound when you move your wrist, but I suggest you include a number of plastic ones to keep the weight of the bracelet light and comfortable.

Tapestry needle, eye-size to accommodate metallic thread
Skein gold-metallic thread, 4 ply
Black elastic waistband, 7 1/2 inches long x 3/4 inch wide
8 assorted gold-metal shank buttons, 1 inch diameter
8 assorted gold-metal shank buttons, 3/4 inch diameter
14 assorted gold-metal shank buttons, 1/2 inch diameter
6 assorted gold-plastic shank buttons, 3/4 inch diameter
5 assorted oval-shaped gold-metal shank buttons,
   3/4 inch wide
12 gold-metal two-hole flat buttons, 3/8 inch diameter
8 inches black flexilace seam binding, 3/4 inch wide
Spool black cotton thread
Standard steel needle, eye-size to choice

✂ Sew the one-inch metal shank buttons to the elastic band at regular intervals, using the metallic thread. Then, in descending-size order, sew down the other shanks to cover the surface of the band evenly, leaving a quarter-inch space bare at each end. Position the buttons to overlap, practically one on top of the other. It's virtually impossible to place them too closely together. As you select each button, juxtapose their sizes and patterns, always considering their colors and textures to complement.

✂ Your sewing knots should be anchored on the topside of the elastic, not the underside, so they won't irritate your wrist when

you wear the finished bracelet. Don't worry about the knots showing: The overlapping layers of buttons will conceal them.

✂ After you have sewed down all of the shanks, fill in any bare spots with the small two-hole buttons. They will sit comfortably beneath the larger buttons.

✂ To line the underside of your bracelet for a finished look, turn the elastic over and loosely whipstitch the lace seam binding in place with cotton thread. Be sure not to stretch out the lace as you sew it on, or the bracelet will become too rigid to fit easily over your hand.

✂ Join the bare ends of the band together, creating a quarter-inch seam. Sew together to form the bracelet. Keep your anchor knot on top. If a bare patch of elastic shows at the join, conceal it by sewing down another button or two.

Gold Button Shoe Ornaments

✂ Coco Chanel would have approved wholeheartedly of these elegant Gold Button Shoe Ornaments. If you wish to coordinate your outfit to a T, select the same buttons you chose for the Bangle Bracelet.

16 gold-metal shank buttons, eight matching pairs,
5/8 inch diameter
8 gold-metal shank buttons, four matching pairs,
1/2 inch diameter

Pair of black grosgrain silk, rosette-style shoe ornaments,
   clip back, 2 1/4 inch diameter
Spool black cotton thread, heavy-weight
Standard steel needle, eye-size to accommodate thread

✀   Of course, the shoe ornaments you create should make a pair, so divide the buttons into two identical groups.

✀   To create the first ornament, sew five of the five-eighths-inch buttons, at regular intervals, around the inner ruffle of the rosette. Snugly fit three of the half-inch buttons to fill the spaces between, overlapping to touch. Sew three five-eighths-inch buttons and one half-inch button to cover the dome center of the rosette. The outer ruffle of the rosette is buttonless for contrast.

✀   Repeat the process for the second ornament.

✀   Present the button bibelots, smartly packed in a four-by-four-by-two-inch white gift box, lined with black tissue. Place the Gold Button Bangle Bracelet into the box and stack the shoe ornaments, one on top of the other, to fill the bracelet's center. Replace the lid and tie a swath of gold organdy ribbon, bundle-style, to finish in a bow with a pouf.

RIGHT ON
THE BUTTON

✂ The ButtonHaus Picture Frame and DecoMetric Pencil Box are equally at home with inspired modern, folk-art, or traditional decor. Turn a workspace into a warm place, and your muse will never be far away. A kaleidoscope of new primary geometrics flashing against aqua green give the desk decorators a vibrant post-Mondrian look.

ButtonHaus Picture Frame

✂ The surprise of pure simplicity is Bauhaus. A fresh palette is key to this project's success. Limit your color choice to the four essentials: red, yellow, blue, purple. Use their full range, the colors should "clash." The hard-edged geometric buttons will set the bright colors off to perfection. To the mix, I added vermilion stars, chartreuse arrows, and my favorite grape-colored stetsons. For added fun and flair, I employed a clever trick of faux: The buttons appear to be hammered in place with tiny brass nails. Actually, they're glued on with bead pins set in the holes to stud the finish.

8 x 10-inch picture frame, unfinished wood,
   3/4 inch wide x 1 inch deep
Fine-grit sandpaper
Tack cloth
Aqua-colored pickling stain, 8 ounces
Sponge brush, 1 inch wide
20 assorted two-hole plastic buttons, geometric shapes,
   primary colors, 1/2 inch to 3/4 inch wide
12 assorted two-hole plastic buttons, geometric shapes,
   primary colors, 1 inch wide
Tube dry-to-clear, plastic-safe glue
64 brass-bead pins
Small wire nipper
Cotton swabs

✄   Remove the glass from the picture frame and set aside to reinsert later. Lightly sand the surface of the frame to smooth away any imperfections. Wipe down with the tack cloth to remove the residue. Apply a thin coat of stain with the sponge brush, following the manufacturer's directions. Set aside in a cool place to dry, about an hour.

✄   Lay the frame on its back. Plan the arrangement before you begin to glue the buttons in place. Use the twenty smallest ones to decorate the front. Pick one for each corner, three to fill the top, three to fill the bottom, and five to run down each side. Mix colors, sizes, and shapes for contrast and balance. The corner buttons look especially nice turned at jaunty angles.

✂ Start with a corner button. Slip a pin through the front of the button. Cut the end off with the nippers to measure flush with the back of the button. Snip the second pin in the same way. Set the pins aside.

✂ Apply a dollop of glue to the corner of the frame. Place the button over the glue and press down, allowing a bit of glue to ooze out the holes. Pick up a trimmed pin with your nippers, and place it in one of the holes. Nudge it to fit snugly and flush with the top of the button. Insert the second pin in the same way. Wipe away any excess glue with a cotton swab.

✂ Repeat the procedure of gluing, snipping, and inserting pins until you have covered the front of the frame. Set aside to dry, about four to six hours.

✂ Stand the frame upright. Choose four large buttons to decorate the top edge. Repeat the process of gluing, snipping, and inserting pins. Set aside to dry, about four to six hours.

✂ Stand the frame on its left side. Choose four large buttons to decorate the right side. Repeat the process of gluing, snipping, and inserting pins. Set aside to dry, about four to six hours.

✂ Stand the frame on its right side and affix buttons to the

left side in the same way as before. Set aside to dry, about four to six hours.

✂ Replace the glass in the frame, *et voilà*! a picture-perfect frame.

DecoMetric Pencil Box

✂ Flash, clash, and contrast the colors and lively geometry of design. The buttons, stain, and pin fittings of the ButtonHaus frame make an encore appearance here. Choose buttons to match, selecting a few sized larger for dramatic contrast. Who knows what strokes of genius will flow from the pen (or pencil) held in this adorable *objet*? Even a grocery list might take on new meaning.

Fine-grit sandpaper
2 1/2 x 2-inch pencil holder, unfinished wood, 4 inches high
Tack cloth
Aqua-colored pickling stain, 8 ounces
Sponge brush, 1 inch wide
4 assorted two-hole plastic buttons, geometric shapes,
    primary colors, 1 1/4 inches wide
20 assorted two-hole plastic buttons, geometric shapes,
    primary colors, 3/4 inch wide
Tube dry-to-clear, plastic-safe glue
48 brass-bead pins
Small wire nipper

✄ Lightly sand the holder, inside and out, to smooth away any imperfections. Wipe down with tack cloth to remove the residue. Apply a thin coat of stain to the inside and the outside with the sponge brush. Set aside in a cool place to dry, about an hour.

✄ Divide your buttons into four groups of six. Each side of the box will require one large button as a design anchor with five smaller buttons arranged around it.

✄ Stand the holder on its side. Start with a center button. Slip a bead pin through the front of the button. Cut the end off with the nippers to measure flush with the back of the button. Repeat the process to cut the length of the second pin. Set the pins aside.

✄ Apply a dollop of glue to the center of the panel. Choose a one-and-one-quarter-inch button. Place it over the glue and press down, allowing a bit of glue to ooze out the holes. Lift a trimmed pin with the nippers, and place it in the hole. Nudge it to fit snugly, and flush with the surface of the button. Insert the second pin in the same way. Wipe away any excess glue. Arrange the smaller buttons around it, three above and two below or two above and three below. Use your good judgment, allowing the geometries of the shapes to suggest a pleasingly balanced design.

✄ Repeat the process of gluing, snipping, and inserting pins to affix the buttons to the remaining three panels of the box. Set aside after you have decorated a panel to allow each side to dry, about four to six hours.

✂ A stained-to-match Wooden In-Box is ideal for presenting these masterpieces. Swathe the gifts in aqua tissue, nestling a bright assortment of unsharpened primary-colored pencils in the tissue-covered holder. Dress it for success in the front page of *The Wall Street Journal*. A power bow is not an option; it's a necessity.

THE BUTTON LOVER'S SOURCE GUIDE

ANIMAIL PET CARE PRODUCTS CATALOG
Box 23547
Chattanooga, TN 37422-3547
(800) 255-3723
•Pet collars and leashes

BALLARD DESIGNS CATALOG
1670 De Foor Avenue NW
Atlanta, GA 30318-7528
(404) 351-5099
•Frames; lamp shades; home furnishings

BANASCH
426 East 6th Street
Cincinnati, OH 45202
(800) 543-0355
•Buttons and notions; fabric and trim

BRITEX
146 Geary Boulevard
San Francisco, CA 94108
(415) 392-2910
•Buttons and notions; fabric and trim

BUTTON SHOP
P.O. Box 1065
Oak Park, IL 60304
(708) 795-1234
•Buttons

BUTTONS AND THINGS FACTORY OUTLET
24 Main Street
Freeport, ME 04032
(207) 865-4480
•Buttons and notions

DISCOUNT CRAFTS SUPPLIES CATALOG
4320 31st Street North
St. Petersburg, FL 33714
(813) 527-4592
•Arts & crafts supplies

EXCLUSIVE BUTTONS
10252 San Pablo Avenue
El Cerrito, CA 94530
(510) 223-1442
•New and vintage buttons

EXPOSURES CATALOG
2800 Hoover Road
Stevens Point, WI 54481
(800) 572-5750
•Frames; assorted containers; lamp shades

FLORIDA JEWELRY CRAFTS, INC
Box 2620 C
Sarasota, FL 34230
(813) 351-9404
•Jewelry supplies

HANDCRAFT FROM EUROPE
1201 Bridgeway
Sausalito, CA 94966
(415) 332-1633
•Buttons and notions; trim

HEARTLAND CRAFT DISCOUNTERS CATALOG
941 South Congress Street
Genesco, IL 61254
(309) 944-6411
•Six thousand arts & crafts items; ribbons of every kind

HOUSE OF CRAFTS AND STUFF
5157 Gall Boulevard
Zephyrhills, FL 33541
(813) 782-0223
•Arts & crafts supplies

KIRCHEN BROTHERS
Dept. C92 Box 1016
Skokie, IL 60076
(312) 676-2692
•Arts & crafts supplies

POTTERY BARN CATALOG
P.O. Box 7044
San Francisco, CA 94120
(415) 421-3400
•All-purpose containers; frames; home furnishings

46

SATIN MOON FABRICS
32 Clement Street
San Francisco, CA 94118
(415) 668-1623
•Buttons and notions; fabric and trim

TENDER BUTTONS
143 East 62nd Street
New York, NY 10021
(212) 758-7004
•New and vintage buttons

VANGUARD CRAFTS, INC. CATALOG
P.O. Box 340170
Brooklyn, NY 11234
(718) 377-5188
•Arts & crafts supplies

ZIMMERMAN'S DISCOUNT CRAFT SUPPLIES
2884 34th Street North
St. Petersburg, FL 33713
(813) 526-4880
•Arts & crafts supplies